The Dumplings Cookbook for Beginners

Irresistible Dumplings Recipes

BY

MOLLY MILLS

Copyright © 2019 by Molly Mills

License Notes

An Amazing Offer for Buying My Book!

Thank you very much for purchasing my books! As a token of my appreciation, I would like to extend an amazing offer to you! When you have subscribed with your e-mail address, you will have the opportunity to get free and discounted e-books that will show up in your inbox daily. You will also receive reminders before an offer expires so you never miss out. With just little effort on your part, you will have access to the newest and most informative books at your fingertips. This is all part of the VIP treatment when you subscribe below.

SIGN ME UP: *https://molly.gr8.com*

Table of Contents

Delicious Dumpling Recipes 7

Recipe 1: Delicious Shrimp Packed Dumplings 8

Recipe 2: Classic Chicken and Dumplings 11

Recipe 3: Easy Rolled Dumplings 14

Recipe 4: Classic Herbed Dumplings 16

Recipe 5: Hearty Pork and Cabbage Dumplings........... 18

Recipe 6: Delicious Mascarpone and Butternut Gnocchi
.... 21

Recipe 7: Czech Style Dumplings with Sauerkraut 25

Recipe 8: Vegetable Style Pan Fried Dumplings 29

Recipe 9: German Style Dumplings.............................. 32

Recipe 10: Classic Pork Dumplings.............................. 34

Recipe 11: Simple Dumplings....................................... 37

Recipe 12: Old Fashioned Dumplings 39

Recipe 13: Traditional Semmelknoedel 42

Recipe 14: Farm House Style Chicken and Drop Dumplings 44

Recipe 15: Turkey Style Dumplings 48

Recipe 16: Filling Potato Dumpling Casserole 50

Recipe 17: Ricotta Style Gnocchi 54

Recipe 18: Simple Potato Dumplings 57

Recipe 19: Simple Gnocchi 59

Recipe 20: Acorn Style Squash Gnocchi Smothered in Parmesan Sage Beurre Blanc 61

Recipe 21: Savory German Style Spaetzle Dumplings . 65

Recipe 22: Filling Potato Dumplings with Onions and Bacon 67

Recipe 23: Savory Dumpling Soup 69

Recipe 24: German Style Kartoffel Kloesse 73

Recipe 25: Sweet Potato Style Gnocchi 75

[5]

About the Author 77

Don't Miss Out! 79

Delicious Dumpling Recipes

AAAAAAAAAAAAAAAAAAAAAAAAAAAAAAAAAAAAAAAAAAAAA

Recipe 1: Delicious Shrimp Packed Dumplings

If you are a huge fan of shrimp and are looking for a healthy and delicious recipe to make, this is the perfect dish to make. These dumplings are plump and juicy, making them extremely satisfying.

Yield: 25 Servings

Cooking Time: 1 Hour

Ingredients for Your Dough:

- ½ Cup of Water, Warm
- ¾ Cup of Starch, Wheat Variety
- 6 Tablespoons of Flour, Tapioca Variety
- 1/8 teaspoons of Salt, For Taste
- 2 teaspoons of Oil, Canola Variety

Ingredients for Your Shrimp Filling:

- ½ Pound of Shrimp, Shelled and Deveined
- 1 teaspoon of Baker's Style Baking Sofa
- 1, 2 Inch Piece of Pork Fatback
- ½ teaspoons of Ginger, Minced
- ½ teaspoons of Garlic, Minced
- ½ teaspoons of Wine, Shaoxing Variety
- ¼ teaspoons of Salt, For Taste
- ¼ teaspoons of Sugar, White
- ¼ teaspoons of Pepper, White in Color and Ground
- 1 teaspoon of Oil, Vegetable Variety
- 1 teaspoon of Cornstarch
- Some Vinegar, Black in Color and for Serving

AAAAAAAAAAAAAAAAAAAAAAAAAAAAAAAAAAAAAAAAAAAAAA

Instructions:

1. The first thing that you want to do is mix all of your ingredients for your filling together in a large sized bowl until thoroughly mixed together.

2. Then mix together all of your ingredients for your dough in a large sized bowl until your mixture forms a sticky dough. Cover with some plastic wrap and set aside for later use.

3. Roll out your dough and cut into small sized wrappers. Fill your wrappers with your filling and fold to seal the edges. Crimp the edges with a fork and sprinkle with some water.

4. Next heat up some oil in a large skillet placed over high heat. Once your oil is hot enough add in your dumplings and cook for the next couple of minutes or until brown in color.

5. Then reduce the heat to low and continue cooking the dumplings for the next 6 to 8 minutes before removing from heat and enjoying whenever you are ready.

Recipe 2: Classic Chicken and Dumplings

This is yet another dumpling recipe that I know you are just going to love making. It is incredibly filling and makes for a great tasting dinner that the entire family will fall in love with.

Yield: 4 to 6 Servings

Cooking Time: 1 Hour and 20 Minutes

Ingredients for Your Chicken:

- 1, 2 ½ Pound Chicken, Cut into Small Sized Pieces
- 3 Ribs of Celery, Finely Chopped and Fresh
- 1 Onion, Large in Size and Finely Chopped
- 2 Bay Leaves, Fresh and Dried
- 2 Bouillon Cubes, Chicken Variety
- 1, 10 ¾ Ounce Can of Cream of Chicken Soup, Condensed
- 1 teaspoon of House Seasoning

Ingredients for Your Dumplings:

- 2 Cups of Flour, All Purpose Variety
- 1 teaspoon of Salt, For Taste
- Some Water, Ice and as Needed

Ingredients for Your House Seasoning:

- 1 Cup of Salt, For Taste
- ¼ Cup of Black Pepper, For Taste
- ¼ Cup of Garlic, Powdered Variety

AAAAAAAAAAAAAAAAAAAAAAAAAAAAAAAAAAAAAAAAAAAAAAAAAA

Instructions:

1. The first thing that you want to do is cook your chicken. To do this place your chicken along with your next 4 ingredients into a large sized pot. Add in four quarts of water and allow your mixture to come to a simmer.

2. Allow your chicken to simmer for the next 40 minutes or until your chicken is completely cooked through. After this time remove the skin from your chicken and return it back to the pot. Keep warm over low heat.

3. Then prepare your dumplings. To do this mix together your ingredients for your dumplings in a large sized mixing bowl. Then use your fingers to knead the dough into a small sized ball and break it off into even sized dumplings.

4. Next add in your soup to your pot with your chicken and allow to continue simmering over low heat.

5. Drop your dumplings into your soup and allow to cook until your dumplings begin to float to the top. That should take about 5 minutes.

6. Remove from heat and served whenever you are ready.

Recipe 3: Easy Rolled Dumplings

If you are looking for a great tasting addition to add to any broth or soup dish that you make, then this is the perfect dish for you to make. Easy to make and absolutely delicious, I know you will want to make it over and over again.

Yield: 7 Servings

Cooking Time: 25 Minutes

List of Ingredients:

- 2 Cups of Flour, All Purpose Variety
- 2 teaspoons of Baker's Style Baking Powder
- 1 teaspoon of Salt, For Taste
- 1/3 Cup of Shortening, Vegetable Variety
- ½ Cup of Milk, Whole
- 2, 14.5 Ounce Cans of Chicken Broth, Homemade Preferable

AAAAAAAAAAAAAAAAAAAAAAAAAAAAAAAAAAAAAAAAAAAAAAAA

Instructions:

1. First combine your first three ingredients together in a large sized bowl. Cut in your shortening and add in enough milk to make a soft dough.

2. Roll out your dough until slightly thick and then cut into small squares.

3. Sprinkle your dough with some flour and drop by the tablespoon into some chicken stock.

4. Cover and allow to boil for the next eight to ten minutes before removing from heat and serving.

Recipe 4: Classic Herbed Dumplings

Here is classic herbed dumpling recipe that I know you are going to love. This is a dumpling recipe that you can make for any soup dish that you make or stew that you want to add a little extra flavor to.

Yield: 6 Servings

Cooking Time: 20 Minutes

List of Ingredients:

- 1 ½ Cups of Flour, All Purpose Variety
- 1 teaspoon of Salt, For Taste
- 1 teaspoon of Baker's Style Baking Soda
- 2 teaspoons of Baker's Style Baking Powder
- 1 teaspoon of Thyme, Dried
- 1 teaspoon of Parsley, Dried
- 1 teaspoon of Oregano, Dried
- 3 Tablespoons of Butter, Soft
- ¾ Cup of Milk, Whole

AAAAAAAAAAAAAAAAAAAAAAAAAAAAAAAAAAAAAAAAAAAAAAAAA

Instructions:

1. Use a medium sized bowl and mix together your first 7 ingredients together until thoroughly combined.

2. Then cut your butter into your mixture until you have a few coarse crumbs in your bowl.

3. Slowly add in your milk and stir until you begin to have a thick batter on your hands.

4. Then drop your batter by the tablespoon into a simmering soup or stew and allow to cook while covered for the next 15 minutes.

5. Serve whenever you are ready and enjoy.

Recipe 5: Hearty Pork and Cabbage Dumplings

Here is yet another Chinese classic dumpling dish that I know you are going to love. It is filled with moist and juicy pork and healthy cabbage that you won't be able to resist.

Yield: 40 to 50 Servings

Cooking Time: 1 Hour

Ingredients for Your Dumplings:

- 1 Pound of Cabbage, Napa Variety and Finely Minced
- 1 tablespoon of Salt, For Taste and Evenly Divided
- 1 Pound of Pork Shoulder, Ground
- 1 teaspoon of Pepper, White in Color and for Taste
- 1 tablespoon of Garlic, Fresh and Minced
- 1 teaspoon of Ginger, Fresh and Minced
- 2 Ounces of Scallions, Minced
- 2 teaspoons of Sugar, White
- 1 Pack of Dumpling Wrappers, 40 to 50 at least
- Some Oil, Canola Variety and for Cooking

Ingredients for Your Sauce:

- ½ Cup of Vinegar, Rice Variety
- ¼ Cup of Soy Sauce, Your Favorite Kind
- 2 Tablespoons of Oil, Chili Variety and Optional

AAAAAAAAAAAAAAAAAAAAAAAAAAAAAAAAAAAAAAAAAAAAAAA

Instructions:

1. The first thing that you want to do is mix all of your ingredients for your filling together in a large sized bowl until thoroughly mixed together.

2. Next roll out your dumpling wrappers and drizzle the edges with some water.

3. Place your filling by the spoonful into the center of your wrappers and cover. Seal the edges with a fork. Repeat with remaining wrappers and filling.

4. Next heat up some oil in a large sized skillet placed over high heat. Once your oil is hot enough add in your dumplings and cook for the next couple of minutes or until brown in color.

5. Then reduce the heat to low and continue cooking the dumplings for the next 6 to 8 minutes before removing from heat and enjoying whenever you are ready.

6. Then mix together all of your ingredients for your dipping sauce in a small sized bowl until evenly mixed together and smooth in consistency. Serve with your dumplings and enjoy.

Recipe 6: Delicious Mascarpone and Butternut Gnocchi

If you are not a huge fan of traditional potato style gnocchi dumplings, then this is a dish that you need to try to make for yourself. This dish features healthy butternut squash and mascarpone cheese, making it a perfect dish to leave you feeling full and satisfied.

Yield: 12 Servings

Cooking Time: 9 Hours

List of Ingredients:

- 1 Pound of Butternut Squash, Fresh
- 1 Cup of Mascarpone Cheese
- ½ Cup of Parmigiano-Reggiano Cheese, Finely Grated
- 2 Eggs, Large in Size and Beaten Lightly
- 1 ½ teaspoons of Salt, For Taste
- ½ teaspoons of Black Pepper, For Taste
- 1 Cup of Flour, All Purpose Variety and Evenly Divided
- ½ Cup of Butter, Unsalted Variety and Soft
- Dash of Cayenne Pepper
- Dash of Salt, For Taste
- Dash of Pepper, For Taste
- ¼ Cup of Sage Leaves, Fresh and Thinly Sliced
- 1 tablespoon of Parmigiano-Reggiano Cheese, Finely Grated

AAAAAAAAAAAAAAAAAAAAAAAAAAAAAAAAAAAAAAAAAAAAAA

Instructions:

1. The first thing you want to do this place your butternut squash into a microwave safe dish and cover with some plastic wrap. Microwave for the next 8 minutes or until tender to the touch. Remove and set aside for later use.

2. Next whisk together your next five ingredients in a large sized bowl until smooth in consistency. Then add in your butternut squash and whisk again until thoroughly blended.

3. Then add in half of your flour and whisk until evenly incorporated. Add in your remaining flour and continue to stir until thoroughly combined. Cover with some plastic wrap and place into your fridge to chill for at least 8 hours.

4. The next day bring a large sized pot of water to a boil. Then use a large sized skillet and melt your butter in it over medium heat.

5. Next scoop out a tablespoon of your butternut mixture and drop it gently into your boiling water. Repeat with remaining mixture until all of your mixture has been used up. Once your dumplings rise to the surface continue to cook for at least one minute in your water and then remove to drain in a plate lined with paper towels.

6. Once drained put your dumplings into your skillet with the melted butter and cook until golden brown in color on each side.

7. Season with your seasonings and garnish with your sage placed on the top. Serve whenever you are ready.

Recipe 7: Czech Style Dumplings with Sauerkraut

This Czech style dumpling recipe is one of the most traditional ways that you can enjoy dumplings today. This is a perfect dish to make for breakfast or for lunch. Either way I know you are going to love it.

Yield: 8 Servings

Cooking Time: 1 Hour and 30 Minutes

List of Ingredients:

- 3 Cups of Flour, All Purpose Variety
- 1 teaspoon of Baker's Style Baking Soda
- 1 teaspoon of Baker's Style Baking Powder
- ½ teaspoons of Salt, For Taste
- ½ teaspoons of Sugar, White
- 3 Eggs, Large in Size and Beaten Lightly
- 1 ½ Cups of Milk, Whole
- 4 Cups of Bread, White, Dry and Cut into Small Cubes
- 4 Slices of Bacon, Sliced into Small Strips
- 1, 16 Ounce Jar of Sauerkraut, Rinsed and Drained
- Dash of Salt, For Taste
- Dash of Pepper, For Taste
- 1 teaspoon of Caraway Seeds
- 2 teaspoons of Water, Cold
- 1 teaspoon of Cornstarch

AAAAAAAAAAAAAAAAAAAAAAAAAAAAAAAAAAAAAAAAAAAAAAAA

Instructions:

1. Use a large sized bowl and mix together your first five ingredients until thoroughly combined.

2. Then make a well into the center of your dough and add in your eggs with your milk. Stir thoroughly to combine and continue to add more milk to make a moist dough.

3. Next add in your white bread and stir enough until your break begins to disappear in the dough.

4. Then bring a large size pot of water to a boil over high heat. While your water is boiling press your dough into a cheesecloth and form it into a loaf shape. Make sure to wrap the cloth around your loaf and tie the ends to seal.

5. Add your loaf to your boiling water and cook for the next 45 minutes making sure to turn your loaf at least halfway through the cooking process. After this time remove from the water and allow to stand to dry for at least 10 minutes.

6. While your loaf is resting fry up your bacon in a small-sized skillet placed over medium to high heat until brown and crispy. Remove from pan and set aside.

7. Add in your sauerkraut and add enough water just to cover the surface. Allow to simmer over medium heat.

8. Add your bacon back into your pan with your remaining ingredients and simmer for the next couple of minutes until thick in consistency.

9. Slice your dumpling loaf and drizzle with your roast drippings and sauerkraut. Enjoy!

Recipe 8: Vegetable Style Pan Fried Dumplings

If you are looking for a healthy dumpling recipe to make, this is the perfect dish for you. It is easy to make and tastes absolutely delicious. I know you are going to love it.

Yield: 24 Servings

Cooking Time: 1 Hour

Ingredients for Your Filling:

- ½ Cup of Carrot, Fresh and Finely Diced
- ½ Cup of Tofu, Five Spice Variety and Finely Diced
- ½ Cup of Seitan, Finely Diced
- ¼ Ounce of Mushrooms, Wood Ear Variety, Dried, Rehydrated and Finely Diced
- 1 Cup of Cabbage, Roughly Diced
- 2 Tablespoons of Garlic, Minced
- 1 tablespoon of Scallions, White Parts Only and Minced
- ½ teaspoons of Sugar, White
- 2 teaspoons of Oil, Sesame Variety

- 2 teaspoons of Soy Sauce, Your Favorite Kind

Ingredients for Your Dumplings:

- ½ teaspoons of White Pepper, For Taste
- ¼ teaspoons of Salt, For Taste
- 2 teaspoons of Cornstarch
- 24 Dumpling Skins, Prepackaged
- 1 tablespoon of Oil, Vegetable Variety

Ingredients for Your Dipping Sauce:

- 1 teaspoon of Oil, Sesame Variety
- 4 teaspoons of Soy Sauce, Light and Your Favorite Kind
- 2 teaspoons of Vinegar, Rice Variety
- 1 Scallion, Finely Sliced

AAAAAAAAAAAAAAAAAAAAAAAAAAAAAAAAAAAAAAAAAAAAA

Instructions:

1. The first thing that you want to do is mix all of your ingredients for your filling together in a large sized bowl until thoroughly mixed together.

2. Next roll out your dumpling wrappers and drizzle the edges with some water.

3. Place your filling by the spoonful into the center of your wrappers and cover. Seal the edges with a fork. Repeat with remaining wrappers and filling.

4. Next heat up some oil in a large skillet placed over high heat. Once your oil is simmering add in your dumplings and cook for the next couple of minutes or until brown and golden in color.

5. Then reduce the heat to low and continue cooking the dumplings for the next 6 to 8 minutes before removing from heat.

6. Then mix together all of your ingredients for your dipping sauce in a small sized bowl until evenly mixed together and smooth in consistency. Serve with your dumplings and enjoy.

Recipe 9: German Style Dumplings

This homemade dumpling recipe is a great dish to make to accompany any soup or chicken recipe that you may make. Feel free to add whatever ingredients you want to this dish to make it truly unique.

Yield: 12 Servings

Cooking Time: 1 Hour and 35 Minutes

List of Ingredients:

- ¾ Cup of Milk, Whole
- ½ teaspoons of Salt, For Taste
- 1 ½ Tablespoons of Flour, All Purpose Variety
- ½ Cup of Water, Cold
- 1 Cup of Flour, All Purpose Variety
- 3 Eggs, Large in Size and Lightly Beaten
- 1 Cup of Flour, All Purpose Variety

AAAAAAAAAAAAAAAAAAAAAAAAAAAAAAAAAAAAAAAAAAAAAAAA

Instructions:

1. The first thing that you will want to do this place your milk and salt into a medium-sized saucepan and heat over medium heat.

2. Then use a small-sized bowl and mix together your flour and water until thoroughly combined.

3. Add into your sauce pan once and once your milk begins to bubble add in your flour mixture and continue to cook until thick inconsistency. This should take at least 2 to 3 minutes. Remove from heat and allow to cool.

4. Once your mixture is cooled fold your eggs into your dough and add in another cup of flour.

5. Drop your dough by the teaspoon into your saucepan and allow to simmer for at least 10 minutes more. Remove from heat and serve whenever you are ready.

Recipe 10: Classic Pork Dumplings

If you are a huge fan of traditional Asian inspired dishes, then this is the perfect dish for you to make. With the help of this recipe you will never have to order traditional pork dumplings from your favorite Chinese restaurant again.

Yield: 70 to 80 Servings

Cooking Time: 30 Minutes

List of Ingredients:

- ½ a Head of Cabbage, Napa Variety and Roughly Chopped
- 1 tablespoon of Salt, For Taste
- 1 Pound of Pork, Ground and Lean
- 1 Cup of Scallions, Sliced Thinly
- ¾ Cup of Cilantro, Fresh and Minced
- 3 Tablespoons of Soy Sauce, Your Favorite Kind
- 1, 2 Inch Piece of Ginger, Fresh and Finely Grated
- 2 Tablespoons of Oil, Sesame Variety
- 2 Eggs, Large in Size and Whisked Thoroughly
- 1, 12 Ounce Pack of Dumpling Wrappers, Round in Size

Instructions:

1. The first thing that you want to do is slice your cabbage and mix it with a touch of salt. Set aside for 5 to 10 minutes. After this time squeeze out the liquid from your cabbage and transfer to another mixing bowl.

2. Mix your cabbage with the rest of your ingredients for your filling until thoroughly combined.

3. Next roll out your dumpling wrappers and drizzle the edges with some water.

4. Place your filling by the spoonful into the center of your wrappers and cover. Seal the edges with a fork. Repeat with remaining wrappers and filling.

5. Then place your dumplings onto a baking sheet and place into your fridge to chill for the next 30 minutes.

6. Next heat up some oil in a large skillet placed over high heat. Once the oil is simmering add in your dumplings and cook for the next couple of minutes or until brown and golden in color.

[35]

7. Then reduce the heat to low and continue cooking the dumplings for the next 6 to 8 minutes before removing from heat and enjoying whenever you are ready.

Recipe 11: Simple Dumplings

If you want yet another traditional dumpling recipe to enjoy, then this is the perfect dish for you. This is as simple as it gets with dumpling recipes, making it the perfect dish to make for a beginner dumpling maker.

Yield: 6 Servings

Cooking Time: 20 Minutes

List of Ingredients:

- 1 Cup of Flour, All Purpose Variety
- 2 teaspoons of Baker's Style Baking Powder
- 1 teaspoon of Sugar, White
- ½ teaspoons of Salt, For Taste
- 1 tablespoon of Margarine, Soft
- ½ Cup of Milk, Whole

AAAAAAAAAAAAAAAAAAAAAAAAAAAAAAAAAAAAAAAAAAAAAA

Instructions:

1. First stir together your first 4 ingredients in a medium sized bowl. Then cut in your butter until your mixture is crumbly.

2. Stir in your milk to make a very soft dough.

3. Drop your mixture by the spoonful into a boiling stew or soup.

4. Cover and allow to cook for the next 15 minutes before serving. Enjoy.

Recipe 12: Old Fashioned Dumplings

With this tasty dumplings recipe, it is a great way to use up any leftover chicken that you may be storing in your kitchen. This dish is one of the most comforting and satisfying dishes that you will ever have the pleasure of making.

Yield: 10 to 12 Servings

Cooking Time: 1 Hour

Ingredients for Your Soup:

- 1, 4 to 5 Pound Chicken, Whole
- 1 Onion, Yellow in Color, Medium in Size and Finely Diced
- 5 Bay Leaves, Fresh and Dried
- 5 Tablespoons of Butter, Unsalted Variety
- 1 ½ Tablespoons of Salt, For Taste
- ½ teaspoons of Black Pepper, For Taste

Ingredients for Your Dumplings:

- 3 Cups of Flour, All Purpose Variety
- 1 ½ teaspoons of Baker's Style Baking Powder
- 1 teaspoon of Salt, For Taste
- ½ Cup of Oil, Vegetable Variety
- ¾ Cup + 2 Tablespoons of Water, Warm
- 2 Eggs, Large in Size and Lightly Beaten
- Dash of Parsley, Minced and Fresh

AAAAAAAAAAAAAAAAAAAAAAAAAAAAAAAAAAAAAAAAAAAAAAA

Instructions:

1. The first thing that you will want to do is make your soup. To do this place your chicken into a large sized soup pot and cover with at least half an inch of water. Then add in your onions and next 4 ingredients for your soup.

2. Cover and allow to cook over high heat until it reaches a boil. Once boiling reduce the heat to low and allow to simmer for the next hour or until your chicken is completely cooked through.

3. Once cooked remove the bay leaves from your pot and transfer your chicken to a cutting board. Shred your chicken finely with 2 forks and then return back to your soup.

4. Next make your dumplings. To do this add in your first 3 ingredients for dumplings into a large sized bowl and whisk thoroughly to blend.

5. Then add in your oil, water and eggs and stir to combine. Knead your dough with your hands until evenly mixed.

7. Next cut your dough into small sized balls and roll out your pieces into thin rectangles.

8. Drop your dumplings into your soup and allow to boil for the next 20 minutes or until your dumplings begin to rise to the surface.

9. After this time remove from heat and garnish with some parsley. Serve while still piping hot.

Recipe 13: Traditional Semmelknoedel

This dumpling recipe is a Bavarian classic that is meant to accompany flavorful dishes such as roasted pork and game dishes dripping in gravy. For the tastiest results I highly recommend that you serve this dumpling dish with some mushrooms and gravy.

Yield: 4 Servings

Cooking Time: 50 Minutes

List of Ingredients:

- 1 Pound of French Bread, Stale and Cut into Small Cubes
- 1 Cup of Milk, Whole
- 2 Tablespoons of Butter, Soft
- 1 Onion, Finely Chopped
- 1 tablespoon of Parsley, Fresh and Roughly Chopped
- 2 Eggs, Large in Size and Beaten Lightly
- Dash of Black Pepper, For Taste
- ½ Cup of Bread Crumbs, Dried

AA

Instructions:

1. First place your bread cubes into a large sized bowl.

2. Then heat up your milk until it begins to boil and pour it over your bread cubes. Stir gently to coat all of your bread cubes and allow to sit for the next 15 minutes.

3. Next melt your butter in a large sized skillet placed over medium heat. Once your butter is melted add in your onions and cook until they are tender to the touch.

4. Then add in your parsley and stir to combine. Remove from heat.

5. Add in your eggs with a dash of salt and pepper into your milk and bread mixture and use your hands to stir thoroughly to combine.

6. Next bring a large sized pot of water to boil and once the water begins to boil drop in your dumplings by the tablespoon until all of your dough has been used up.

7. Continue to cook for the next 20 minutes before removing with a spoon and serving whenever you are ready.

Recipe 14: Farm House Style Chicken and Drop Dumplings

Here is yet another soup style recipe that I know you are going to want to make. The best thing about this recipe is that you can easily put it together when you are running tight on time.

Yield: 10 to 12 Servings

Cooking Time: 1 Hour and 45 Minutes

Ingredients for Your Chicken Soup:

- 2, 3 Pound Chickens, Cut into Small Sized Pieces
- ½ Cup of Butter, Unsalted Variety and Soft
- 6 Carrots, Medium in Size and Chopped into Small Pieces
- 6 Cloves of Garlic, Sliced Thinly
- 4 Stalks of Celery, Chopped into Small Pieces
- 2 Leeks, Large in Size, White Part Only, chopped into Small Pieces and Soaked
- 2 Onions, Yellow in Color, Medium in Size and Chopped Finely
- 1 tablespoon of Seasoning, Poultry Variety
- ½ Cup of Flour, All Purpose Variety

Ingredients for Your Dumplings:

- 2 ½ Cups of Flour, All Purpose Variety
- ¾ Cup of Milk, Whole and as Needed
- 2 Tablespoons of Butter, Soft
- 1 tablespoon of Baker's Style Baking Powder
- 2 teaspoons of Salt, For Taste
- 2 Eggs, Large in Size and Beaten Lightly
- ¼ Cup of Parsley, Fresh and Roughly Chopped

Instructions:

1. The first thing that you want to do is make your soup. To do this place your chicken into a large sized pot filled with at least 16 cups of water and bring it to a boil. After this time reduce the heat to low and allow your chicken to cook for the next 25 to 30 minutes or until completely cooked through. After this time remove your chicken and set aside for later use.

2. Once your chicken is cool to the touch shred your chicken finely with two forks and set aside.

3. Use another medium sized pot and melt your butter over medium heat. Once your butter is fully melted add in your next 6 ingredients and stir to combine. Cook for the next 8 to 10 minutes or until your vegetables are tender to the touch.

4. Then add in your flour and stir to combine.

5. Next make your dumplings. To do this use a medium sized bowl and add in all of your ingredients for your dumplings. Mix until thoroughly combined.

6. Then cut your dough into smaller sized balls and drop into your soup to cook for the next 10 to 12 minutes or until they begin to float to the surface.

7. Remove from heat and serve with a garnish of parsley and enjoy.

Recipe 15: Turkey Style Dumplings

If you are looking for a way to spice up your next Thanksgiving meal, then this is the perfect dish to do it with. These dumplings are packed full of delicious flavor that I know you won't be able to get enough of.

Yield: 10 Servings

Cooking Time: 1 Hour and 10 Minutes

List of Ingredients:

- 1 Pound of Turkey, Fully Cooked and Finely Chopped
- 3 Cups of Water, Warm
- Dash of Salt, For Taste
- Dash of Pepper, For Taste
- 3 Tablespoons of Flour, All Purpose Variety
- 1, 12 Ounce Pack of Biscuit Dough, Refrigerated

AAAAAAAAAAAAAAAAAAAAAAAAAAAAAAAAAAAAAAAAAAAAAAAA

Instructions:

1. First place your first 4 ingredients into a medium sized saucepan and bring your mixture to a boil. Once your mixture is boiling reduce your heat to low and simmer for the next 30 to 40 minutes.

2. Next spread your flour on a medium sized cutting board and roll out your dough. Cut into small sized pieces and drop these into your broth.

3. Cook over low heat for the next 40 minutes before removing from heat and serving.

Recipe 16: Filling Potato Dumpling Casserole

If you need to feed a large group of people, then this is one dish that you will want to make. Feel free to double up on the amount of sauce and cheese that you use to make it truly unique.

Yield: 6 Servings

Cooking Time: 1 Hour and 15 Minutes

List of Ingredients:

- 2 Cups of Potatoes, Mashed Thoroughly
- 1 Cup of Flour, All Purpose Variety
- 2 Eggs, Large in Size and Lightly Beaten
- 1 ½ teaspoons of Salt, For Taste
- 1/8 teaspoons of Black Pepper, For Taste
- 1 Onion, Medium in Size and Finely Chopped
- 3 Tablespoons of Butter, Soft
- 2 Tablespoons of Flour, All Purpose Variety
- 1 Cup of Cream, Light
- 1 Cup of Broth, Chicken Variety and Homemade Preferable
- ½ Cup of Parmesan Cheese, Freshly Grated
- ½ Cup of Jarlsberg Cheese, Finely Shredded

AAAAAAAAAAAAAAAAAAAAAAAAAAAAAAAAAAAAAAAAAAAAAA

Instructions:

1. Use a medium sized bowl and mix together your first 5 ingredients until thoroughly blended together. Place this mixture into a plastic bag and seal.

2. Bring a large size pot of water to boil over high heat. Then drop in spoonsfuls of your mixture from your plastic bag into the water and allow to cook for the next 10 minutes or until your dumplings begin to rise to the top. Once the dumplings have risen remove from your pot and set aside to drain.

3. Once your dumplings are drained thoroughly place them into a large sized baking dish.

4. Then preheat your oven to 350 degrees.

5. While your oven is heating up melt your butter in a large sized skillet placed over medium heat. Once your butter is melted add in your onions and cook for the next 10 minutes or until they are tender to the touch.

6. Add in your next three ingredients and continue cooking until thick in consistency.

7. Remove from heat and add in at least half of your parmesan cheese and half of your Jarlsberg. Stir until smooth in consistency. Pour this mixture over your dumplings and sprinkle with remaining cheese.

8. Place into your oven to bake for the next 45 minutes or until your dumplings are golden brown in color.

9. Remove from oven and allow to cool slightly before serving.

Recipe 17: Ricotta Style Gnocchi

If you are craving Italian, then this is a delicious dumpling recipe that you need to try for yourself. In order to make great tasting Gnocchi, make sure that you dry your ingredients thoroughly before using them.

Yield: 5 Servings

Cooking Time: 1 Hour

Ingredients for Your Gnocchi:

- 1, 8 Ounce Container of Ricotta Cheese
- 2 Eggs, Large in Size and Beaten Lightly
- ½ Cup of Parmesan Cheese, Freshly Grated
- 1 teaspoon of Salt, For Taste
- 1 teaspoon of Pepper, For Taste
- 1 teaspoon of Garlic, Powdered Variety
- 1 Cup of Flour, All Purpose Variety and as Needed

Ingredients for Your Sauce:

- 3 Tablespoons of Olive Oil, Extra Virgin Variety
- 1 tablespoon of Garlic, Minced
- 1, 15.5 Ounce Can of Tomatoes, Finely Diced
- Dash of Red Pepper Flakes, Crushed and Optional
- 6 Leaves of Basil, Finely Shredded
- Dash of Salt, For Taste
- Dash of Pepper, For Taste
- 8 Ounces of Mozzarella Cheese, Fresh and Freshly Grated

AAAAAAAAAAAAAAAAAAAAAAAAAAAAAAAAAAAAAAAAAAAAAAAA

Instructions:

1. The first thing that you will want to do is stir together your first 6 ingredients in a large sized bowl until evenly combined. Then add in your flour and any additional flour that you may use until you make a soft dough.

2. Next divide up your go into 4 equal sized pieces and roll to 4 even sized ropes on a floured surface. Cut these ropes into 1-inch pieces and place on to a baking sheet that is lightly floured. Then lace into your fridge to chill.

3. Next heat up your oil in a large sized saucepan. Once your oil is hot enough add in your garlic and cook until they are soft. Add in your tomatoes and red peppers and bring this mixture to a simmer. Continue to cook for the next 10 minutes.

4. Add in your basil and season with a touch of salt and pepper.

5. While your sauce is simmering bring a large sized pot of salted water to a boil over high heat. Once your water is boiling add in your gnocchi and cook for the next 2 minutes. Drain after this time.

6. Stir your mozzarella cheese into your sauce and allow the cheese to soften up. Pour into a serving bowl and add in your gnocchi. Serve whenever you are ready.

Recipe 18: Simple Potato Dumplings

If you are looking for a quick and simple way to feed your family, this is the perfect recipe for you. I know that once you get a taste of it yourself, this will become a family favorite in your household.

Yield: 6 Servings

Cooking Time: 30 Minutes

List of Ingredients:

- 1 Cup of Potato Flakes, Instant Variety and Mashed
- 1 Cup of Water, Hot
- 1 teaspoon of Salt, For Taste
- 2 Eggs, Large in Size and Beaten Lightly
- ¾ Cup of Flour, All Purpose Variety

AAAAAAAAAAAAAAAAAAAAAAAAAAAAAAAAAAAAAAAAAAAAAA

Instructions:

1. Use a large sized mixing bowl and whisk together your first 3 ingredients. Allow your mixture to sit for the next 10 minutes before adding in your eggs and flour. Stir again to combine.

2. Then place your dough onto a lightly floured surface and knead for a couple of minutes.

3. Next bring a large saucepan filled with water to a boil over high heat. Separate your dough into 7 equal sized dumplings and drop them into the water to boil for the next 20 minutes or until they begin to rise to the top of the water.

4. Remove your dumplings from your water and set aside to drain. Serve whenever you are ready.

Recipe 19: Simple Gnocchi

This simple and easy dumpling recipe is made using flour, egg and potatoes, making it one of the easiest recipes to make. It is traditionally passed down through generations, but now you have access to it to make it a great addition to nearly any meal that you make.

Yield: 4 Servings

Cooking Time: 1 Hour

List of Ingredients:

- 2 Potatoes, Whole
- 2 Cups of Flour, All Purpose Variety
- 1 Egg, Large in Size and Beaten Lightly

AAAAAAAAAAAAAAAAAAAAAAAAAAAAAAAAAAAAAAAAAAAAA

Instructions:

1. First bring a large sized pot of water to a boil over high heat. Add in your potatoes and cook until they are slightly tender. This should take about 15 minutes. Drain and mash thoroughly with a fork.

2. Then combine your mashed potato mixture with your egg and flour in another large sized bowl. Knead thoroughly until a soft dough begins to form.

3. Shape smaller portions of your dough into long size ropes and cut them into half-inch pieces.

4. Bring another large sized hot of water to a boil and drop in your dumplings. Cook for the next 3 to 5 minutes or until your dumplings have risen to the top. Drain and serve whenever you are ready.

Recipe 20: Acorn Style Squash Gnocchi Smothered in Parmesan Sage Beurre Blanc

This is a perfect gnocchi recipe to make during the autumn months. It is a creative way to cook traditional dumplings that is smothered in some Parmesan sage sauce.

Yield: 8 Servings

Cooking Time: 1 Hour and 20 Minutes

List of Ingredients:

- 1 Squash, Acorn Variety, cut into Halves and Seeded
- 2 Cloves of Garlic, Pressed Firmly
- ½ teaspoons of Salt, For Taste
- 1 Egg, Large in Size and Beaten Lightly
- 1 Cup of Flour, Whole Wheat Variety
- 1 Cup of Flour, All Purpose Variety
- 7 Cups of Water, Warm
- 1 tablespoon of Salt, For Taste
- 1 Cube of Bouillon, Chicken Variety
- 1 Cup of Beer, Your Favorite Kind
- 1/3 teaspoons of Sage, Rubbed
- ¼ teaspoons of Black Pepper, For Taste
- ¼ Cup of Butter, Cold and Cut into Small Cubes
- ½ Cup of Parmesan Cheese, Freshly Grated

AAAAAAAAAAAAAAAAAAAAAAAAAAAAAAAAAAAAAAAAAAAAAAA

Instructions:

1. First cook your squash in a microwave for the next 10 minutes or until tender to the touch.

2. After this time mash your squash thoroughly and then add in your next five ingredients until your dough is sticky.

3. Then turn your dough onto a lightly floured surface and roll into thin and long ropes. Then chop your dough into smaller pieces to 4 more dumplings.

4. Next bring a large pot of water to a boil over high heat and add in your dumplings, one at a time and cook until they begin to float to the top. Once floating remove from your pan and set aside.

5. Once your dumplings are cooked drain the water from your pot and then return it to heat. Add in your next 4 ingredients and bring your mixture to a boil. Allow your mixture to continue boiling for the next 15 minutes before reducing the heat to low.

6. Whisk in your butter until thoroughly melted and then add in your dumplings. Allow to cook for the next 10 minutes or until your dumplings are brown in color.

7. Remove from heat and serve with some Parmesan cheese. Enjoy.

Recipe 21: Savory German Style Spaetzle Dumplings

If you wish to enjoy a German style dumpling recipe, this is the perfect dish for you. For the tastiest results I highly recommend cooking your Spaetzle in bacon drippings instead of butter.

Yield: 6 Servings

Cooking Time: 20 Minutes

List of Ingredients:

- 1 Cup of Flour, All Purpose Variety
- ¼ Cup of Milk, Whole
- 2 Eggs, Large in Size and Beaten Lightly
- ½ teaspoons of Nutmeg, Ground
- Dash of Pepper, White in Color and For Taste
- ½ teaspoons of Salt, For Taste
- 1 Gallon of Water, Hot
- 2 Tablespoons of Butter, Soft
- 2 Tablespoons of Parsley, Fresh and Roughly Chopped

AAA

Instructions:

1. The first thing that you will need to do is mix together your first 4 ingredients.

2. Then beat together your eggs with your milk and add it into your dry ingredients. Mix until smooth in consistency and thoroughly combined.

3. Drop your dough by the tablespoon into some simmering liquid and cook for the next 5 to 8 minutes. After that time drain and serve whenever you are ready with a garnish of parsley.

Recipe 22: Filling Potato Dumplings with Onions and Bacon

Once you make this dish for yourself the first time, I guarantee that you will want to make it over and over again. For the tastiest results I highly recommend serving this dish with some beef or roasted pork roast.

Yield: 6 Servings

Cooking Time: 1 Hour and 10 Minutes

List of Ingredients:

- 2 Potatoes, Large in Size, Peeled and Finely Chopped
- 2 Eggs, Large in Size and Beaten Lightly
- Some Flour, All Purpose Variety and as Needed
- ¼ Pound of Bacon, Finely Chopped
- ½ of an Onion, Large in Size and Finely Chopped

AAAAAAAAAAAAAAAAAAAAAAAAAAAAAAAAAAAAAAAAAAAAAAAAA

Instructions:

1. First bring a large sized pot of water to a boil over high heat. Season with a touch of salt.

2. Then place your potatoes into a food processor and pulse until finely chopped. Add in your eggs and continue to pulse for a few minutes or until thoroughly combined. Pour this mixture into a large sized bowl and add in enough flour to make a thick and sticky dough.

3. Next drop your dough by the tablespoon into your boiling water and allow to boil for the next 20 minutes or until they begin to flow to the top. Once floating remove your balls from the water and set aside to drink.

4. Next place your onions and bacon into a large sized to skillet placed over medium heat. Allow to cook for the next 10 minutes or until your bacon is brown and crispy.

5. Then place your dumplings into the pan and cook until brown on each side.

6. Remove from heat and serve while still piping hot. Enjoy.

Recipe 23: Savory Dumpling Soup

If you are looking for a savory and filling soup dish to make when you are feeling under the weather, this is the perfect dish for you. It is very easy to make and makes a great dish to make to help you feel better.

Yield: 6 Servings

Cooking Time: 50 Minutes

List of Ingredients:

- 1 ½ Cups of Flour, All Purpose Variety
- 1 teaspoon of Baker's Style Baking Powder
- 1 teaspoon of Salt, For Taste
- 1 tablespoon of Oil, Vegetable Variety
- 1 Egg, Large in Size and Beaten Lightly
- ¾ Cup of Water, Warm and as Needed
- 6 Potatoes, Medium in Size, Peeled and Cut into Small Sized Cubes
- 1 teaspoon of Salt, For Taste
- 8 Cups of Water, Warm
- 2 Tablespoons of Butter, Soft
- 4 Ounces of Bacon, Finely Diced
- 1 Onion, Large in Size and Finely Chopped

AAAAAAAAAAAAAAAAAAAAAAAAAAAAAAAAAAAAAAAAAAAAA

Instructions:

1. First use a medium sized bowl and combine in your first three ingredients together until thoroughly combined. Then add in your egg with some water and whisk thoroughly with a fork into your flour mixture. Continue to mix until a soft dough begins to form. Cover your dough and set aside to rise.

2. Next place your potatoes into a large sized pot with boiling water and boil for the next 10 to 15 minutes or until they are tender to the touch.

3. Next melt your butter in a large sized skillet placed over medium heat. Once your butter is melted add in your bacon and onions and cook until your onions are golden in color and your bacon is fully cooked.

4. Next chop your dough into small pieces and drop them into your boiling water that you cooked your potatoes in. Cook for the next 10 minutes or until your dumplings begin to float to the top.

5. Then use a large sized skillet and add in your bacon and onions along with your dumplings. Pour this mixture into your soup mixture and allow to rest for couple minutes before serving. Enjoy.

Recipe 24: German Style Kartoffel Kloesse

Here is yet another German inspired dish to make traditional potato dumplings. Feel free to make this as a side dish or a main entrée. Either way I know you are going to love it.

Yield: 12 Servings

Cooking Time: 30 Minutes

List of Ingredients:

- 9 Potatoes, Medium in Size and Peeled
- 1 teaspoon of Salt, For Taste
- 3 Eggs, Large in Size and Beaten Lightly
- 1 Cup of Flour, All Purpose Variety
- 2/3 Cup of Bread Crumbs, Dried
- ½ teaspoons of Nutmeg, Ground
- 1 Cup of Butter, Soft
- 2 Tablespoons of Onion, Finely Chopped
- ¼ Cup of Bread Crumbs, Dried

AAAAAAAAAAAAAAAAAAAAAAAAAAAAAAAAAAAAAAAAAAAAAAA

Instructions:

1. The first thing you want to do to place your potatoes in a large sized pot of water and bring to a boil. Cook for the next 20 minutes or until your potatoes are soft to the touch. Once tender remove from water and drain.

2. Next mash your potatoes thoroughly, making sure to leave them somewhat lumpy.

3. Add in your next 5 ingredients until thoroughly mixed. Then using your hands roll your dough into even small sized balls.

4. Bring another large sized pot of water to a boil and season with some salt. Once boiling gently drop in your dumplings into the water and allow them to cook for the next 3 minutes or until they begin to rise to the surface. Remove after this time and set aside for later use.

5. Then bring a large sized skillet over medium heat and add in your butter. Once your butter is melted add in your onions and breadcrumbs and cook for the next 5 minutes or until tender to the touch. Remove from heat and pour sauce over your cooked dumplings. Serve whenever you are ready and enjoy.

Recipe 25: Sweet Potato Style Gnocchi

This recipe is a delicious and unique twist on traditional gnocchi. I highly recommend pairing this dish up with your favorite kind of alfredo sauce and butternut squash for the tastiest results.

Yield: 4 Servings

Cooking Time: 1 Hour and 5 Minutes

List of Ingredients:

- 2, 8 Ounce Sweet Potatoes, Scrubbed
- 1 Clove of Garlic, Pressed Firmly
- ½ teaspoons of Salt, For Taste
- ½ teaspoons of Nutmeg, Ground
- 1 Egg, Large in Size and Beaten Lightly
- 2 Cups of Flour, All Purpose Variety

AAAAAAAAAAAAAAAAAAAAAAAAAAAAAAAAAAAAAAAAAAAAA

Instructions:

1. The first thing that you will want to do is preheat your oven to 350 degrees. Once your oven is hot enough bake your sweet potatoes for the next 30 minutes or until they are soft to the touch. Remove from the oven and set aside to cool completely.

2. Once your sweet potatoes are cool peel them and mash them thoroughly with a fork.

3. Add in your next 4 ingredients and stir thoroughly to combine. Add in your flour and continue to stir until you have a soft dough.

4. Next bring a large sized pot of water to a boil and drop in your dough by the tablespoon. Cook until your dumplings began to float to the surface and then remove from the water. Serve whenever you are ready and enjoy.

About the Author

Molly Mills always knew she wanted to feed people delicious food for a living. Being the oldest child with three younger brothers, Molly learned to prepare meals at an early age to help out her busy parents. She just seemed to know what spice went with which meat and how to make sauces that would dress up the blandest of pastas. Her creativity in the kitchen was a blessing to a family where money was tight and making new meals every day was a challenge.

Molly was also a gifted athlete as well as chef and secured a Lacrosse scholarship to Syracuse University. This was a blessing to her family as she was the first to go to college and at little cost to her parents. She took full advantage of her college education and earned a business degree. When she graduated, she joined her culinary skills and business acumen into a successful catering business. She wrote her first e-book after a customer asked if she could pay for several of her recipes. This sparked the entrepreneurial spirit in Mills and she thought if one person wanted them, then why not share the recipes with the world!

Molly lives near her family's home with her husband and three children and still cooks for her family every chance she gets. She plays Lacrosse with a local team made up of her old teammates from college and there are always some tasty nibbles on the ready after each game.

Don't Miss Out!

Scan the QR-Code below and you can sign up to receive emails whenever Molly Mills publishes a new book. There's no charge and no obligation.

Sign Me Up

https://molly.gr8.com

Printed in Great
Britain
by Amazon